MARY JANE

Watching the Disciples

Learning From Their Mistakes

A LENTEN STUDY FOR ADULTS

ABINGDON PRESS / Nashville

WATCHING THE DISCIPLES:
LEARNING FROM THEIR MISTAKES

Copyright © 2008 by Abingdon Press

This book is printed on acid-free paper.

Library of Congress Cataloging-in-Publication Data on file

ISBN 978-0687-64788-0

All scripture quotations unless noted otherwise are taken from the New Revised Standard Version of the Bible, copyright © 1989 by the Division of Christian Education of the National Council of the Churches of Christ in the United States of America. Used by permission. All rights reserved.

08 09 10 11 12 13 14 15 16 17 — 10 9 8 7 6 5 4 3 2

MANUFACTURED IN THE UNITED STATES OF AMERICA

Contents

Introduction

Have you ever locked your keys in the car or locked yourself out of the house? Have you ever lost your temper with a family member or a good friend? If you have made any of these mistakes, did you make it only *once* in your life? If you shake your head as you recall making these or similar mistakes over and over again, you immediately realize how difficult is the task of learning from your own mistakes. Consider also how many times you said to yourself that you would "never say *that*"—"that" being your mother's or father's most frequent criticism—to your own child. Remember how you felt the first time you heard the very same words coming from your own mouth!

Surely, learning from *someone else's* mistakes is even more difficult! Sometimes another person's mistake is so shocking and terrible that it does shake us and cause us to change our own behavior. Most of the time, however, we are reluctant to look for ourselves in the circumstances of someone else's mistake. We either ignore the errors of others or we assume we would never make the same bad choices. Nevertheless, the premise of this book is that we *can* learn from the mistakes of others.

What do we mean by the word *mistake*? A mistake involves thinking or saying the wrong thing, doing the wrong thing, or not doing what is expected in a particular context. A mistake is not the same thing as a sin, although some mistakes may be sinful. For example, when you were in school and made errors on your math test, you made mistakes. Certainly no one would label these errors as sins (although a particularly demanding teacher may have made you feel as though they were!). People who lie, steal, or commit murder will sometimes confess, "I made a mistake." Certainly *these* mistakes are also considered sins.

This Lenten study looks at the twelve disciples as they tried to follow Jesus and live the challenging life to which he had called them. Based on Gospel texts, each chapter focuses on one mistake the dis-

5

ciples made, usually one for which they received correction or a reprimand from Jesus. For the disciples, expectations for their behavior were based on what Jesus taught them and demonstrated to them by his example. Some of the disciples' mistakes would not have been labeled as such apart from the context of being followers of Jesus. A few of their errors would be considered wrong in any context. Most of these mistakes result from the disciples' missing the point of Jesus' teaching, preaching, and example. The mistakes treated in this study are not an exhaustive list of everything the disciples did wrong, but they were selected based on having application to contemporary experiences and being particularly suited for our Lenten focus.

Too often we overlook the disciples, assuming that their lives are not instructive for us or thinking that their experiences as first-century followers of Jesus are not relevant for contemporary discipleship. Another possibility is that we hear these names as saints—Peter, Matthew, John, and others—holy men whose exemplary lives we cannot match. Alternatively, we may, without much reflection, read particular episodes in the Gospels in which the disciples have key roles and label their behavior or questions as misguided at best or, at worst, just plain stupid. We ask, "How could they live with Jesus day after day and yet fail to understand?" We may shake our heads at their foolish mistakes, confident that we would never repeat them. While the truth of the character of these men lies somewhere between exemplary saint and bumbling, ineffective follower, we may not have taken the time to discover and explore an accurate picture of them.

The aim of this study is to connect more closely with the disciples and to see in them many of our own failings. This will require both seeing them as the ordinary men that they were and reflecting more broadly on the particular mistakes we observe. The task will not always be easy. At times, what Jesus criticizes as a mistake may be hard to accept. Furthermore, hearing his reprimands and corrections as words directed not only to the disciples but also to us may make us very uncomfortable.

On Ash Wednesday, you may receive ashes on your forehead and hear the call to a time of repentance. The season of Lent is an appropriate time for penitence, and for introspection and reflection on our relationship with God. Examining the mistakes of the Twelve can help us to assess our own discipleship in order to see where it may need correcting and strengthening. Jesus was a persistent and forgiving teacher of the Twelve. No matter how many mistakes the disciples made, Jesus did not dismiss them to return to their previous professions. He never gave up on them. As he was faithful to them, so will he be with us so long as we keep showing up for his lessons. During these weeks of Lent, we hope to find guidance for our pilgrimage. Come along as we join the Twelve in their on-the-job-training to become disciples of Jesus.

Questions for Reflection and Discussion

1. What do you know about the twelve disciples? How many can you name? Can you recall any stories that you think illustrate some or all of the disciples making a mistake? (Use your Bible and other resources as needed to locate stories about the twelve disciples and refresh your recollection.) What do you think Jesus was looking for in choosing his disciples? What is it about the Twelve that made them particularly suitable, or not so suitable, for the vocation to which they were called?

2. What does Lent mean to you? In what ways do you hope to deepen your relationship with God during this Lenten season? Can you identify a particular mistake in your own discipleship that you would like to correct?

3. Read Luke 5:1-11. In this story of the call of some of the disciples, note particularly Simon Peter's initial responses to Jesus both before and immediately after putting out the nets. How might these reactions to Jesus be labeled as mistakes? Describe Simon Peter's actions after expressing his initial questions and fears.

Prayer

On this first day of Lent, O God, we profess our commitment to an intentional season of prayer and meditation, of confession and repentance.

We long to be more faithful and authentic disciples of Jesus.

We confess that we have made this commitment before and not often succeeded.

Make our hearts and souls eager for more intimate time with you.

Challenge us to return to our Lenten path, even when we realize we have walked away from it for a time.

Open our minds to let the Gospel stories of the disciples be fresh, instructive, and compelling for our own discipleship.

Call us to a sacrificial journey for these forty days.

Amen.

Enough: Five Loaves and Two Fish Are Not Enough

Scripture: Read Matthew 14:13-21.

How many times do we ask the question, "How much is enough?" We may be packing clothes for a long vacation, saving for our retirement, or contributing to our church when we wonder what is enough. The question is often difficult to answer in part because the concept of "enough" is subjective, varying across persons and circumstances. Concern with how much was enough arose often as Jesus tried to teach his disciples. At times, the Twelve accepted Jesus' assessment of "enough"; but on some occasions, they made mistakes.

When Jesus sent the disciples out to preach and heal, he gave them specific instructions about what was enough to carry with them: "He ordered them to take nothing for their journey except a staff; no bread, no bag, no money in their belts; but to wear sandals and not to put on two tunics" (Mark 6:8-9). Certainly their provisions were stark! However, the Gospel writers recorded no complaint from the disciples in response.

How were they to survive the journey when they took so little of what they needed? Jesus instructed them to accept hospitality in the towns they visited. He wanted the disciples to travel lightly not only to facilitate their ease in moving from place to place, but also to instill in them the need for community and for dependence on God.

9

In addition, those extending hospitality would have the benefit of participating in Jesus' ministry by caring for and being with the disciples. Perhaps had the disciples carried "enough" in the usual sense—enough money, bread, and clothing—they might have missed important lessons about humility, trust, and gratitude. Nevertheless, this experience did not prepare the disciples for the challenge Jesus gave them to provide enough food for a hungry crowd.

All four Gospels include the story of Jesus feeding five thousand men, along with uncounted women and children (Matthew 14:13-21; Mark 6:30-44; Luke 9:10-17; John 6:1-14). In Matthew (15:29-39) and Mark (8:1-10), a second feeding of about four thousand people is also reported. Thus the Gospels contain six quite similar accounts of large crowds being fed by Jesus. The unusual repetition alone makes the story significant among those told about him.

In the first story, Jesus had been teaching and healing throughout the day when the disciples came to him saying, "This is a deserted place, and the hour is now late; send the crowds away so that they may go into the villages and buy food for themselves" (Matthew 14:15). Probably the disciples assumed that the thousands gathered there were as hungry and tired as they were. Furthermore, they may have thought that Jesus had done enough for one day. The disciples' advice to Jesus may have conveyed a "let's-call-it-a-day" message.

Jesus agreed with the disciples' assessment that everyone needed to eat. He surprised them, however, when he told them his plan: "You give them something to eat" (14:16). We can imagine the tone with which the disciples replied as they looked out over the crowd. Perhaps they were incredulous or a bit frustrated as they responded, "We have nothing here but five loaves and two fish" (14:17). Alternatively, they may have replied sarcastically, "Are we to go and buy two hundred denarii worth of bread, and give it to them to eat?" (Mark 6:37). The disciples' estimate of the cost of feeding bread to the crowd was about two hundred times a typical daily wage of one *denarii*. We can understand their "you've-got-to-be-kidding" attitude!

Were the disciples referring to their own provisions when they reported about the loaves and fish? If so, they may have been reluctant to offer the food they had brought for themselves. Perhaps they thought, "Why should we give up *our* food, which we need? What good would our sacrifice do, anyway?" Nevertheless, they gave the bread and fish to Jesus. After making the crowd sit down, Jesus blessed, broke, and gave the food to the disciples, who gave it to the people. The food was enough. As Matthew records, all the people ate until they were satisfied; then, the disciples collected twelve baskets full of leftover bread and fish.

Perhaps the disciples' first mistake was that they wanted to send the crowd home. Although the disciples thought that the people had been there long enough and that Jesus had done enough for them, Jesus thought otherwise. He wanted the people to stay, to sit down, and to eat, perhaps in part for the value of the fellowship among them. With five thousand people spread out in the deserted place, only some in the crowd could witness each healing. Probably many could not hear all of the teaching throughout the day. Perhaps Jesus knew that the experience was not enough until the people sat down in the community of smaller groups where they could share the stories of those who were healed, and repeat and debate the teaching they had heard. Being "filled" required more than bread alone. The time of fellowship helped the people better understand, appreciate, and remember all they had experienced. Maybe new supportive relationships were begun among those who chose to follow Jesus.

The more obvious mistake of the disciples, however, was their assumption that what they had was not enough. Certainly a crowd of five thousand to feed would be overwhelming to anyone, particularly when the dinner party was unexpected! Little surprise, then, that the provisions the disciples had seemed pitiful in the face of what was needed. All they could suggest was buying food for everyone, a plan immediately dismissed as extravagant and unreasonable. The disciples had no vision or creativity in approaching the challenge they faced. Even so, the disciples could be seen as pragmatic and their advice to Jesus as appropriate. After all, Jesus cautioned about carefully calculating the costs of a large undertaking. He asked, "For which of you, intending to build a tower, does not first sit down and estimate the cost, to see whether he has enough to complete it?" (Luke 14:28). The disciples appeared to make a quick calculation of the cost of feeding the crowd and decided they could not do it.

Before condemning the disciples for their lack of faith, look more closely at how Jesus dealt with them. In response to the disciples' recommendation to send the crowd away, Jesus replied simply, "You give them something to eat" (Matthew 14:16). While we cannot know Jesus' tone, much less his intent, we can speculate that he spoke gently in a matter-of-fact voice, perhaps even lifting his eyebrows as if his statement were a question, or a sly suggestion. The disciples' quick response seemed to indicate that they thought Jesus' idea was the most ridiculous thing they had ever heard! With a reply that sounds calm to our ears, Jesus told the men to bring what food they had to him. Could he have said this with a smile and a sigh? Again, we certainly do not know, but clearly Jesus did not reprimand them in any way. On other occasions, Jesus' words to his disciples sounded angry or disappointed or frustrated. This time, Jesus did not fuss at the disciples for lacking the wisdom to know what he would do or the faith to believe what he could do. Perhaps Jesus did not expect them to know how to handle this seemingly overwhelming task. This time, he taught the disciples by example, showing them how he could use what was available to satisfy the crowd.

The disciples' "mistake" was not a sinful act that deserved punishment. This episode was just another step, perhaps a stumble, along the road toward learning to be a disciple. Once Jesus told the disciples what to do next—"bring me what you have"—they did it. They did not argue with his instruction. Furthermore, they followed his directions to make the people sit down, to pass out the food, and later to gather the leftovers. As we focus on the disciples' mistakes, we do not want to minimize what they do that is right. In this case, although they probably continued to ponder questions and concerns about what Jesus told them to do, they were nevertheless obedient to him.

What application can this dramatic story have for our lives? Perhaps recognizing the disciples' mistake in assuming that the crowds had been with Jesus long enough can remind us of the benefit of sharing in smaller groups within our faith communities. Listening to a profound sermon may have a powerful impact at the moment, but by the time we get home from church we may be unable to recall the details. By the next day, all we can say for sure is that the sermon was "really good." While this may be enough to get us back to church the next Sunday, it may not help us be better disciples during the week. Sharing our reactions to and questions about what we have heard may be essential to our understanding of teaching and preaching. Often the disciples came to Jesus when they did not understand his teaching. Here, they made a mistake in not recognizing that the small-group experience that *they* needed in order to process what they heard would be needed by others listening to Jesus.

Consider now the primary mistake made by the disciples in assessing what was enough. Have we ever thought that a need was so great, given our limited resources, that we threw up our hands and did nothing? We may observe a growing number of homeless persons in our community needing food and shelter, or children in our schools needing health insurance to receive adequate medical care. A natural disaster may leave hundreds or even thousands of people without anything beyond the clothes on their backs. Outside our borders, civil war may leave tens of thousands in refugee camps without adequate food or clean water. The needs so overwhelm us that we may agree with the attitude we speculated the disciples having—*giving all I have will not solve the problem and would only include me among the needy.* What can we learn from the disciples' mistake?

The few loaves and fish were enough only after Jesus somehow multiplied the food. Although perhaps not in exactly the same way, multiplying available resources can happen in our own experience. For example, a church member describes the needs of a family whose home has burned down. He puts some money in a basket and starts passing it among the people. Others take out their wallets, and soon the basket is full of bills and coins and checks and pledges written on scraps of paper. Let's not make the mistake of assuming that because what we have is not enough to solve a problem that we need not do anything. Let's invite other persons to share what they have too. We can't ignore the need for resources to be blessed and multiplied in order to be adequate.

The disciples thought that the only way to feed the people was to buy food, and that was way too expensive. We, too, need to look beyond an obvious, but impractical, solution. For example, while buying health insurance is one way to get healthcare for children in a community, that solution is too expensive for almost all individuals and most churches. Instead of giving up, look for more creative possibilities. Working with healthcare professionals, hospitals, and churches in the area to establish a free medical clinic for children may be part of a solution. Lobbying government to extend health insurance at reduced rates to low-income families may help. Certainly options partnering private and public sectors are available.

Finally, what can we learn from observing Jesus' response and the disciples' actions? Perhaps we may feel called to address an over-whelming problem. Questioning that call is not wrong, and, in fact, is probably appropriate and necessary. But, if we continue to discern the validity of the call, we need to look for the first step and take it. What we learn from the disciples, on this occasion and many others, is that they kept showing up and doing what Jesus asked them to do. That was enough for Jesus this time. That is all God will ask of us as well.

The disciples made a mistake in believing that their resources were not enough for what needed to be done. Furthermore, they over-looked the need for the people to stay around a while and talk. Surely we can identify with both mistakes. We, too, may want to send peo-ple away at the end of an exhausting day. Looking at overwhelming need in our own community and around the world, we, too, think that what we have is not enough. Rather than dismissing the feeding stories as miracle events without practical application for our lives, we can search for their meaning today. During this season of Lent, we can focus not only on intentional personal sacrifice but also on inten-tional giving to others. We can hear Jesus' words to his disciples as a call to us: "You give them something to eat" (Matthew 14:16).

Questions for Reflection and Discussion

1. Read Matthew 15:32-39, an account of a second feeding of thousands. Compare and contrast this account with the first feeding story in Matthew 14:13-21. Did the disciples learn from their first mistake? Propose some explanations for their behav-ior in this second story.

2. Lent is a season for sacrifice. Have you or would you consider giving up something for Lent? How might our small sacrifices relate to and remind us of Jesus' concept of "enough"?

3. How does the culture around us determine or influence our view of what is "enough"? Reflect on or discuss some specific examples.

4. List a few specific questions that you have asked related to the issue of "enough." What guidelines or criteria do you use in assessing what is enough in your own life or that of your family?

5. Identify one local or global "overwhelming" need. Propose a

first step that has the potential to be blessed and multiplied so as to make a significant contribution to alleviating the need.

Prayer

O God, quiet the noise around us and within us so that we can be attentive to your presence as we begin this Lenten journey.

Help us during the coming weeks to claim the discipline we need, but so often lack, to live out the desire of our heart and soul for a meaningful season of sacrifice and preparation.

We confess that we live as if we never have enough—not enough to satisfy our "needs," much less to satisfy our wants.

Forgive us for thinking that the emptiness we feel inside can be filled by acquiring more things on the outside.

Challenge us to look at what we have and see that it is enough, not only for *our* needs but also to share with others.

We acknowledge what we know but so often forget—

Only in receiving your grace and love, O God, can we be satisfied in the depth of our souls and say, "It is enough."

Amen.

Focus for the Week

Be attentive to bread this week. Let it remind you of having *enough* relative to the needs of a hungry world; and let it symbolize for you the Bread of Life, which is truly enough.

Status: Climbing the Ladder of Success?

Scripture: Read Mark 9:33-41; 10:35-45.

Among the first men whom Jesus called to be disciples were four fishermen—the brothers Simon (who was renamed Peter) and Andrew, and the brothers James and John, sons of Zebedee. Simon Peter owned a boat (see Luke 5:3), while the Zebedee brothers, who were in business with their father, hired other men to work with them (see Mark 1:20). Nevertheless, we can assume that both fishing businesses were quite modest. Neither family ran a major shipping enterprise. The evidence in the Gospels suggests that these were hardworking men with little status in the community.

Jesus also called the tax collector Levi (see Mark 2:14; note that Levi is called Matthew in Matthew 9:9). Members of this profession generally were despised for their dishonest practice of collecting more tax than was due and pocketing the excess. Even if he obtained considerable income this way, Levi was an outcast without respect or status.

The professions of the other disciples are not known. Probably they practiced trades that provided income for little more than basic necessities. None was an educated religious leader or wealthy landowner. When the disciples left all they had to follow Jesus, they were not sacrificing expectations of wealth or status in the commu-

17

nity. Their prospects for success certainly would not be any brighter following a relatively unknown, small-town prophet! However, despite their modest backgrounds and their willingness to follow an even more uncertain path, the disciples (or at least some of them) soon revealed a desire for recognition and reward. On at least four occasions, the disciples looked and sounded like contemporary "climbers" up the "ladder of success." The disciples' mistakes on these occasions were particularly significant, because Jesus so clearly rejected, and even preached the reversal of, societal views on who should come first and last.

On one occasion, Jesus and his disciples had just arrived in Capernaum when Jesus asked the men, "What were you arguing about on the way?" (Mark 9:33). Perhaps the color drained from their faces in that tense moment as they remembered their argument about "who was the greatest" (v. 34). The disciples had observed Jesus' devotion to societal outcasts and his challenges to rich and powerful people with high status. They had heard Jesus pronounce "woe to you who are rich" and "woe to you when all speak well of you" (Luke 6:24, 26). They knew Jesus called followers to "deny themselves" and to "lose their life for [his] sake" (Mark 8:34-35). How could they argue about who was the greatest among them? Their behavior was disappointing at best and disgusting at worst. They did not answer Jesus' question.

The disciples, young men probably in their twenties or thirties, formed the inner circle around a charismatic man whose preaching and healing drew growing crowds. Perhaps their experience was somewhat like that of young people who become attracted to a promising politician. One day they are listening intently to the inspiring, but relatively unknown, leader who has a fresh vision for the country, and two years later they are heading up campaign headquarters for this same person, who is now a leading presidential candidate. "Pumped" by these heady experiences, the young men and women jockey for positions in the campaign and argue at times about who would be best to fill hoped-for positions on a presidential staff.

Were the disciples vulnerable to letting Jesus' popularity go to their heads? Perhaps they thought Jesus needed a representative to respond to requests from influential people who asked Jesus to heal someone or have dinner or speak in their synagogue. Would the "greatest" have more authority and be the "go to" man under Jesus?

We cannot know exactly what "being the greatest" meant to the disciples, but the context suggests that earthly ambition led them to argue over status within their group. As they followed Jesus on the road that day, the disciples competed to claim, "I'm number one!"

The disciples made a mistake when, not as a passing temptation but as a desire worthy of an argument, they wanted to be great. When Jesus confronted them, they made no attempt to explain but froze in guilty silence. Nevertheless, instead of rebuking them, Jesus called them over and taught them, saying, "Whoever wants to be first must be last of all and servant of all" (Mark 9:35). Then, calling a child to him, Jesus said, "Whoever welcomes one such child in my name welcomes me, and whoever welcomes me welcomes not me but the one who sent me" (Mark 9:37). Jesus' representative was a child, who, in that culture, was not valued or respected or granted any status at all. That a child should be held up as a model of "greatness" was inconceivable to the disciples.

The issue of status was apparent on a second occasion, when an exorcist was successfully casting out demons in Jesus' name, a good work the disciples could not denounce. John complained to Jesus, saying, "Teacher, we saw someone casting out demons in your name, and we tried to stop him, because he was not following us" (Mark 9:38). The disciples were angry that this man, who was not one of Jesus' followers, had infringed on their exclusive right to Jesus' name and authority. Perhaps the primary motivation in the disciples' action was their jealousy of this exorcist's success in light of their own recent failure to exorcise a demon from an epileptic boy (see Mark 9:14-29). Preventing the success of another is one way to get ahead in the quest for higher status. Once again, the disciples had made a mistake.

Jesus responded clearly: "Do not stop him" (Mark 9:39). What? Shouldn't Jesus be angry about this imposter? Why would he allow an outsider to use his name to claim power against demons? Jesus explained, "Whoever is not against us is for us" (Mark 9:40). Jesus did not demand recognition as a superior exorcist or exclusive rights to power to do good deeds. Although the religious leaders had tried to discredit *him* by accusing him of casting out demons under the authority of Satan, Jesus did not similarly condemn this other exorcist. He wanted God's will and God's work to be done, and he welcomed anyone to participate in that agenda.

A third mistake occurred when James and John came to Jesus with a special request. They opened with a bold statement, saying, "Teacher, we want you to do for us whatever we ask of you" (Mark 10:35). (We can wonder what Jesus' immediate reaction was to this remark; we would surely be put on guard by such a beginning!) The brothers then made their request: "Grant us to sit, one at your right hand and one at your left, in your glory" (Mark 10:37). These two seats traditionally were considered to be the places of honor, power, and influence. This mistake by the disciples was so similar to the previous argument over greatness that one wonders if these two men had paid attention to Jesus' instruction then. We do not know what sort of "glory" the brothers were anticipating Jesus would attain, only that they wanted to share in it. Jesus told James and John that they did not know what they were asking, and Jesus questioned whether they could "drink the cup" that he would drink (Mark 10:38). James and John confidently said that they could, although they did not yet understand what sort of suffering Jesus was implying.

When the other disciples heard James and John's request, another argument ensued. We can identify with the anger of the other ten disciples: If we virtuously resisted asking to sit next to the guest of honor, we might be resentful of someone else who did ask. Aware of the anger, jealousy, and resentment brewing among the disciples, Jesus once again explained the nature of the life to which he had called them, saying, "Whoever wishes to become great among you must be your servant, and whoever wishes to be first among you must be slave of all" (Mark 10:43-44).

One final episode about status, found only in the Gospel of John, is a poignant story. At the last meal he would share with the Twelve, Jesus took a towel and a basin of water and began to wash the disciples' feet. Only a servant would kneel on the floor and perform this lowly task. When Peter's turn came, he asked, "Lord, are you going to wash my feet?" (John 13:6). Since Jesus had already washed the feet of some of the other disciples, his intention to continue was obvious. Probably Peter's tone communicated more than his words. Although Jesus indicated that he would understand later, Peter said to Jesus, "You will never wash my feet" (John 13:8). Peter did not want the leader he followed to be his servant. Perhaps he reacted in part out of the realization of how low his own status must be if he followed a lowly servant.

Once Jesus insisted that to have a "share with" him, he would have to wash Peter's feet, the impulsive disciple asked for a full bath: "Lord, not my feet only but also my hands and my head!" (John 13:9). Perhaps Jesus looked at this disciple and shook his head, or smiled, before explaining that a bath was not needed. After washing the feet of Peter and the remaining men, Jesus explained that his actions were an example for them to wash others' feet, to be servants. Jesus must have hoped that the disciples would remember this humbling experience and finally learn the lesson.

As the disciples tried to learn a radically different way of living, they not only made mistakes, but also repeated them even after correction. We likely recognize our own tendency to make the same mistake over and over again. We make resolutions never to do something, we read self-help books about our weakness, or we seek advice and support. Still, we slip up again. For the disciples, letting go of their desire for recognition and status was a difficult task. Can we identify with them? Perhaps we might accept a new job because of the prestige of the firm, the job title, or the size of the office, acknowledging our new position unlikely will be as rewarding in other important ways as our current job. Seeking to improve our status may influence our choice of clothes, car, cell phone, hairstylist, or neighborhood. It may determine the friends or church we choose. Pursuing status is not a meaningful life goal, and it may require sacrifice of a satisfying vocation or of one's values. Such a pursuit can breed jealousy and resentment, which can damage relationships.

Jesus told his disciples, "The least among all of you is the greatest" (Luke 9:48). Who are the least in our society? Perhaps Jesus would put before us the high-school dropout loading the dishwasher in a fast-food restaurant, or the immigrant lawn maintenance worker who does not speak English. These "invisible" people are similar in societal status to a child in Jesus' day. Certainly Jesus' perspective on being "great" is radically different from that in our culture. Aligning our wants and behavior with Jesus' teaching and example is difficult.

What possible identification can we have with the disciples' trying to stop the exorcist? Do we dismiss or demean "competing" Christian communities whose beliefs and practices are very different from ours? Are we even more likely to reject the good works of other religious groups who not only practice their faith differently but also call God by a different name? If, instead, we relate to other faith communities in the spirit of "whoever is not against us is for us," how might we act? What results would follow if we partnered with other churches, whether more "liberal" or "conservative" than our own, in local service projects or in disaster-relief efforts outside our community? And what if we were to consider inviting not only Christian congregations but also Jewish, Muslim, and others to join us in honoring a national day of prayer or in seeking solutions to community problems?

When Jesus washed the disciples' feet as a symbol of servanthood, he told them to do likewise. If we take this call seriously, where do we go, and what tasks do we undertake? A servant may provide care for an Alzheimer's patient or a disabled child, perhaps providing respite for a caregiver. Washing the clothes of persons who are homeless, providing cold water for volunteer homebuilders on a hot afternoon, or taking food to a grieving family may be "foot-washing" experiences. Remaining as a valued teacher in a school located within a low-income neighborhood rather than accepting an offer at an elite private academy might be considered a servant action. Certainly, no willing servant lacks for jobs needing to be done.

Trying to attain a higher status was a mistake for the disciples. Jesus called them, and us, not to "greatness" as it is traditionally understood, but to be "servant of all" (Mark 9:35). He did not say, however, that we should deny our gifts or refuse the best job offer in our chosen vocation. Jesus used his gifts as teacher, preacher, and healer. He attracted large crowds who praised him, and he dined with persons of prestige and influence. Jesus did not, however, seek title or power or wealth. He ministered to the outcasts, and his words and actions eventually made enemies of the religious leaders. To discern the difference between offering the best of our talents and energy to God and trying to achieve greatness requires constant reflection on Jesus' teaching and example, and it also requires consistent self-examination. As we continue on our Lenten journey, we may want to begin a regular practice of questioning our motives: Are we humbling or exalting ourselves? Are we seeking the seats of honor? Are we trying to be first, to be great, or are we assuming the role of servant?

As we look at the disciples, we easily see their mistakes. The challenge is to recognize similar mistakes in our actions and to take seriously Jesus' instruction: "Whoever wants to be first must be last of all and servant of all" (Mark 9:35).

Questions for Reflection and Discussion

1. Some contemporary Christian preachers and teachers are well-known and earn high incomes from television programs and best-selling books. Compare the recognition and status of the disciples to that of religious leaders today. Reflect on or discuss how receiving such recognition may or may not be a mistake.

2. Many organizations and institutions print the names of donors grouped by categories, based on the amount of their contributions. What are the positive and negative aspects of this practice? Should churches adopt this practice? Why or why not?

3. The disciples felt threatened by the good works of someone who was not part of their immediate faith community. What do you perceive as being threatening to the beliefs or practices of your faith community? What is the basis for your perception? Jesus said, "Whoever is not against us is for us"; reflect on your perception in light of Jesus' statement.

4. Can you identify in your life a frequent purchase, buying habits, or regular activities that reflect a desire for acquiring status above "the least of these"? In what ways might you consider adjusting your purchasing habits or your activities during Lent as an intentional response to Jesus' call to be servant to all?

5. Have you ever been a participant in a foot-washing? If not, try to imagine how you might feel as a participant in this practice. Which experience did you, or would you, find more difficult—washing another person's feet or having your feet washed? Explain your answer. Read John 13:14; how might we interpret for ourselves Jesus' call to his disciples in this verse? (Another way of putting this question might be, What would this level of Christian servanthood look like in your own life?)

Prayer

Fill our hearts, O Lord, with the desire to be servants, in the way Jesus taught us and showed us.

Trouble us to look intentionally for "the least of these" in our community.

Direct us to our own path of servanthood.

Give us strength and commitment to pursue that path amidst the pressure to compete for prestige, power, and wealth.

Help us, O God, to recognize all others who are "for you" and to accept and support gracefully their faithful witness.

Amen.

Focus for the Week

Look for ways this week to respond to the call to forgo status and be a servant.

Agenda: Listen to *Our* Plan for You, Jesus

Scripture: Read Matthew 16:21-26; John 11:1-16.

Before beginning his ministry, Jesus went into the wilderness for a time of testing. (See Matthew 4:1-11; Mark 1:12-13; Luke 4:1-13.) The Gospel writers described his experience as a series of temptations by Satan. During this time, Jesus discerned, or at least began to discern, the nature of his vocation. Jesus' "agenda" was to follow God's call to teach, heal, and preach the good news of the kingdom of God. Throughout his ministry, Jesus was encouraged, or perhaps even tempted, by his followers to pursue agendas that did not match God's plan for him. Although none was described so dramatically as the wilderness temptation, these other challenges to follow a different path were significant, and they surely made Jesus' sticking to his own agenda more difficult. Perhaps the occasions when Jesus escaped from the crowds to pray were at least in part due to his need to continue to discern the path of his calling and to receive strength from God to continue his journey.

In Mark's Gospel, immediately following his appearance in Galilee to begin his ministry, Jesus called his first disciples. The appropriate role for a disciple was implicit in Jesus' call as he said, "Follow me" (Mark 1:17). The disciples were called to follow—to walk behind, figuratively if not literally. They were not called to lead, because they did not know the way. Several times, however, the disciples suggested,

25

even demanded, an agenda for Jesus that reflected their own desires and goals.

On at least two occasions, the disciples tried to protect Jesus from physical danger. Certainly their desire to keep Jesus safe was not inherently wrong. Nevertheless, they made a mistake when they presumed to have better judgment than Jesus in determining where he should go and what he should do. What made Jesus' decision-making about the pursuit of his agenda more reliable than that of the disciples? As we noted, Jesus spent time in the wilderness sorting out his own calling, and time in prayer discerning the steps of that path. He talked with the disciples about his calling. Early in his ministry, he avoided dangerous situations. Only later did he knowingly take considerable risk. If someone has followed these steps—observing an intentional time of discernment, engaging in constant prayer (with questioning and listening rather than telling), having discussion with close friends, and taking intentional and carefully examined steps along the chosen path—then our respect and support may more appropriately be given.

The first time Jesus talked to his disciples about his expected suffering, death, and resurrection (see Matthew 16:21), one disciple reacted strongly. "Peter took him aside and began to rebuke him, saying, 'God forbid it, Lord! This must never happen to you' " (16:22). Peter thought he knew what was best for Jesus. His intention could be considered noble. He wanted to protect Jesus from harm, certainly from pain, suffering, and death. Again, this mistake was not inherently a bad thing.

Additional context may be helpful in appreciating Peter's boldness. Prior to Jesus' words about his suffering and death, Peter had confessed that Jesus was the Messiah. Jesus responded by affirming Peter, proclaiming him the rock, the foundation, of his church and further said, "I will give you the keys of the kingdom of heaven, and whatever you bind on earth will be bound in heaven" (Matthew 16:19). Perhaps Peter thought he had been delegated more authority than Jesus intended. Maybe Peter thought that he had been authorized to be the disciple in charge. In this light, Peter may appear slightly less impulsive or inappropriate. But perhaps Peter instead had his mind not only on Jesus' safety but also on Jesus' success. Suffering and death were *not* on the path toward the kind of successful "kingdom" that Peter hoped they were pursuing, so Peter's agenda may have included less-noble aims than Jesus' protection.

In response to Peter's strong words, Jesus returned the rebuke, saying, "Get behind me, Satan! You are a stumbling block to me; for you are setting your mind not on divine things but on human things" (v. 23). Jesus implicitly accused Peter of trying to be the leader. In calling him Satan, Jesus did not mean that Peter was evil. Perhaps he was suggesting that Peter was tempting him, as Satan had in the wilderness, toward a different path than the one God had called him to follow. Furthermore, Jesus rebuked Peter for giving priority to safety —a human thing—over God's call to Jesus—a divine thing. Perhaps at times Jesus struggled to keep following the difficult path he chose. He may have been disappointed, even resentful, when the disciples made the path even more difficult by demanding that he abandon it. He needed for them to be supportive, not to impose obstacles.

On another occasion much later in Jesus' ministry, the disciples similarly tried to protect Jesus from danger. In a story found only in John (11:1-44), Jesus received word from his friends Mary and Martha that their brother, Lazarus, was ill. The two women wanted Jesus to come to Bethany to heal Lazarus. Bethany was in Judea, near Jerusalem. Just prior to this event, Jesus had been in Jerusalem at a Jewish festival (see John 10:22-23). While in the Temple, Jesus had so angered his listeners that they "took up stones again to stone him" (John 10:31). This had, in fact, been attempted on another occasion (see John 8:59). Little wonder, then, that the disciples would not be eager to go near Jerusalem.

Two days after receiving the message from Mary and Martha, Jesus told his disciples that they were going to Judea. The disciples responded, "Rabbi, the Jews were just now trying to stone you, and are you going there again?" (John 11:8). Jesus gave a cryptic reply. (See John 11:9-10.) Whatever their interpretation of Jesus' words, the disciples understood that he was overruling their concern and reluctance. Once again, their trying to protect Jesus from danger was a mistake. The disciples quickly moved from reluctance to bravado. In words that will be repeated by all the disciples in later, and far more threatening, circumstances, Thomas spoke here for the group, saying, "Let us also go, that we may die with him" (John 11:16).

On each of these occasions, the disciples revealed their desire to protect Jesus and, no doubt, to ensure their own safety as well. Also hidden beneath the call for safety was probably some motivation for achieving their view of success. In the next two examples, the disciples tried to impose their agenda on Jesus by seeking retribution or trying to retaliate against enemies of Jesus.

In a story recorded only in Luke (9:51-56), Jesus and his disciples had begun their journey to Jerusalem. Messengers sent by Jesus to a Samaritan village up ahead were turned away. On seeing this, James and John asked Jesus, "Lord, do you want us to command fire to come down from heaven and consume them?" (v. 54). In response, Jesus "rebuked" the two disciples. James and John had an agenda that included violent retribution against those who did not receive Jesus and their entire group. This was a mistake. Clearly, violence was not Jesus' agenda.

The second example was perhaps a feeble attempt by the disciples to protect Jesus, but was more likely retaliation borne out of anger when threatened with defeat and possibly death. In this example, Judas, one of Jesus' twelve disciples, in betrayal of Jesus, has brought a large crowd of representatives of the chief priests and elders to the place where Jesus has been praying in the company of the other disciples. The leaders of this crowd intend to arrest Jesus and take him into custody. All four Gospel stories of Jesus' arrest note that someone drew a sword and struck the slave of the high priest, cutting off his ear. The Gospel of Matthew indicates that a disciple was responsible for this deed (see Matthew 26:51-54), while the Gospel of John specifically names Peter as the one (see John 18:10-11).

Certainly Peter's temperament, his impulsiveness and bravado as revealed in earlier stories, make him a likely choice for the one with the sword. If Peter was once again pursuing his agenda of trying to protect Jesus, surely he saw that his efforts were too little, too late. If he was retaliating in anger, perhaps he could see that this one slave was not the source of the danger in which they found themselves. Peter's primary mistake was in thinking that Jesus would want him to use force for any reason. Jesus cautioned the disciples against violence, saying, "Put your sword back into its place; for all who take the sword will perish by the sword (Matthew 26:52). In a different response recorded in John—"Put your sword back into its sheath. Am I not to drink the cup that the Father has given me?" (18:11)—Jesus emphasized his need to follow his agenda and not that of the disciples. In this tense situation at the time of Jesus' arrest, Peter's agenda for Jesus and himself resulted in violent retaliation. In the same situation, Jesus appeared neither frustrated nor angry. The disciples had not accepted, much less supported, Jesus' agenda. Thus, they fought, or they acted as if they wanted to do so, and then they fled.

Can we identify with the disciples as they mistakenly tried to impose their agenda on Jesus? Sometimes we think we know better than our spouse or our child or our friend what she should be doing with her life, or he with his. Like the disciples, we presume that our agenda is better, and we are quite willing to try to impose it. Alternatively, we may have had experiences where someone else tried to change who we are and what we think we are called to be. Many conflicts in relationships are the result of one person or both trying to impose agendas on the other. Such behavior can cause disappointment, depression, anger, and resentment.

We acknowledge that not every path chosen by every individual is God's will. People do make mistakes in discerning God's leading, while others do not listen at all for a word from God. We may be confident that we know that our family member or friend is making a bad decision in the job they are planning to accept, or regarding the person whom they have chosen to marry, or the potentially dangerous mission they are intending to pursue. If we are being asked to support someone who is seeking our approval, we need to counsel that person to listen, ask, and pray. We need to do the same before responding.

The disciples tried to protect Jesus from danger, even if they were also protecting themselves or their own best interests. You may have faced a young family member or friend who wants to volunteer for some type of service, relief, or missionary work in potentially dangerous countries. Even if this young person has done considerable research on the risks, is well-trained for the work, has talked with representatives of the sponsoring organization, and has sought the wise counsel of experienced participants in similar work, might a concerned parent or friend still express reservations or ask their young person not to go? We do not want the people we love to take dangerous risks. We want to protect them. We may not fully understand or appreciate the call and commitment they feel, as surely as the disciples did not understand Jesus' commitment to his path. In such cases, we need to pray, asking God for strength and guidance in seeking to offer support for the other person's agenda.

Again, like the disciples, do we ever lash out in frustration and anger over the choices others make? We might not draw a sword, and hopefully we would not consider calling down fire from heaven! Nevertheless, there may be occasions where we have retaliated with destructive words and perhaps damaging actions—words and actions that may be just as fruitless and foolish as those of Peter. On such occasions, if we had sought to listen, understand, and be accepting of the chosen path of the other person, we might not have reacted with anger when that person continued to follow his or her agenda.

We need to be very careful about projecting our understanding, our vision, or our agenda on those around us. If God is working in someone's life, let God work. We are not called to stand in the way. Again, however, we need to be helpful in the person's discernment that the path being followed is indeed God's will. We *should* challenge paths that seem contrary to God's call and question paths that seem clearly not to fit the person's abilities and gifts. However, such challenges must be made respectfully and carefully.

Finally, we need to consider whether we impose *our* agenda—rather than God's agenda—upon *ourselves*. We cannot use the claim that we have no idea what God wants us to do as an excuse to walk or run down any path we choose. God calls us to love God and to love our neighbor as we love ourselves. Throughout the Gospels, Jesus teaches and demonstrates the specifics of how we can interpret and enact those two commands. Imposing our own selfish agendas on our lives, in spite of our knowing in mind and heart that we are not living the life to which we have been called, is perhaps the most destructive agenda of all.

As you continue this Lenten journey, consider trying to put aside your concern with the agendas of those around you. Focus instead on God's agenda for you. Let these remaining weeks be a time of intentional discernment of some aspect or next step of God's call to you.

Questions for Reflection and Discussion

1. Give examples of ways we may try to impose our agenda on family members, on friends, or within our church community. What are some ways to distinguish between exerting appropriate leadership or guidance, and inappropriately imposing our own agenda?

2. Read Mark 1:32-39 and 9:2-8. Speculate on the agendas behind Peter's (Simon's) actions or suggestions to Jesus in each of these stories.

3. What are some ways to challenge family members, church leaders, government officials, or business leaders about their agendas?

4. What can we learn from Jesus' example about how to discern God's agenda for our lives?

5. The writer suggested that the disciples had an agenda for a successful ministry that was different from the plan Jesus was pursuing. Compare and contrast Jesus' ministry with the "successful" ministry the disciples seem to desire. Reflect on the agenda of your own church or of some broader group of Christian churches. What characterizes "success" or "successful" ministry in these churches?

6. Reread John 11:1-16. Identify the mistake the disciples made in assuming that Jesus meant his words literally. What other occasions can you identify or recall where the disciples and other listeners misunderstood Jesus' metaphorical language?

Prayer

So many times we have said, "Let Thy will, not my will, be done."

But we confess, O God, that the words of our mouths may not be the meditation of our hearts.

We say to others, and to ourselves, that we are searching for your will.

Yet, while Jesus spent forty days in obedient discernment and testing, we find spending forty minutes a week in prayer difficult.

We focus our energy on redirecting someone else's agenda.

We pursue our agenda for our own lives, assuming that what we want is what you want.

31

Forgive us, O God.

As we continue on this Lenten journey, call us into our own wilderness to reflect on your will.

Quiet our distractions so that we can listen to you.

Remind us daily of the agenda to which you have called us:

To love you with all of our heart, soul, mind, and strength;

And to love our neighbors as we love ourselves.

Give us strength to pursue these commandments.

Amen.

Focus for the Week

As you consult your calendar for your daily agenda, be reminded of Jesus' agenda for you as his disciple.

Cost: We Will Follow You Wherever You Go

Scripture: Read Luke 14:25-33; Mark 10:17-31.

Throughout his ministry, Jesus cautioned his disciples, other followers, and would-be followers about the high costs of discipleship. He never offered an encouraging "Come on; it's easy; anyone can do it!" Quite the contrary, Jesus talked about the difficult sacrifices required for discipleship. On one occasion, he said that his disciples would hate their family members and "even life itself" (Luke 14:26). Although Jesus was not commanding us to "hate" our spouse, children, and others as we understand that emotion, he was cautioning that discipleship needed to take precedence over conflicting obligations, even to family. He continued, saying, "Whoever does not carry the cross and follow me cannot be my disciple" (v. 27). Jesus concluded by saying that his disciples must give up all their possessions (v. 33). Accepting these job requirements was costly for the Twelve, and it certainly would be so for us.

When Jesus called Peter, Andrew, James, and John to follow him, they sacrificed their livelihood, walking away from their fishing boats and nets (see Matthew 4:18-22). Although they occasionally may have used their boats to fish or to provide transportation for Jesus and their fellow disciples, for the most part they became dependent upon the hospitality of others. The disciples also left their homes and families, at least during most of their time with Jesus. Similarly, when

Jesus called the tax collector Levi, he immediately left his booth and followed Jesus (see Luke 5:27-28). From the limited information in the Gospel accounts about the personal lives of these five disciples, as well as the other seven, we may assume that they incurred the costs that Jesus outlined—they abandoned family and possessions.

Unlike the Twelve, several would-be disciples whom Jesus called were not willing to make the sacrifice he required. The best known of these was the rich man who asked Jesus about inheriting eternal life (see Mark 10:17-22). Perhaps perceiving the rich man as somewhat disingenuous in his questioning, Jesus fired back, "You know the commandments..." (v. 19). The rich man proudly responded that he had kept them all. Perhaps he was more interested in receiving public recognition of his righteousness than in becoming a disciple. His confidence that he was an outstanding applicant was a big mistake. Jesus confronted the man with a conditional call: "You lack one thing; go, sell what you own, and give the money to the poor, and you will have treasure in heaven; then come, follow me" (v. 21). The cost of discipleship was shocking to this rich, young ruler, who "went away grieving, for he had many possessions" (v. 22).

After the rich man left, Jesus remarked to his disciples about the difficulty wealthy people have in entering God's kingdom. With his famous hyperbole about it being like a camel going through a needle's eye, Jesus stressed that doing so was almost impossible. The disciples were "astounded" at what Jesus had said and asked, "Then who can be saved?" (Mark 10:26). While the rich ruler made the bigger mistake, the disciples were also mistaken about the cost. They were shocked that Jesus would require so much from the ruler. Perhaps they were dissatisfied with who and how many would be excluded from discipleship if Jesus set the standard so impossibly high. Peter spoke for the disciples, saying to Jesus, "Look, we have left everything and followed you" (Mark 10:28). Maybe Peter was not so sure what he would have done had he been very rich. Nevertheless, he had walked away from what he *did* have, so he wanted to be sure Jesus recognized that! Jesus acknowledged the costs they all had incurred in leaving their homes, their families, and more, and he promised them that they would receive "a hundredfold now in this age...and in the age to come eternal life" (Mark 10:30).

Given the evidence that they did leave jobs, family, and home, how can we label any aspect of their behavior in this context as a mistake? In fact, the disciples did underestimate other costs of discipleship, and they found themselves unable to meet threats and challenges that no doubt they had hoped, and even expected, they could endure.

Think about the physical and emotional stress the disciples faced in following Jesus. They followed a demanding teacher who regularly challenged them mentally and in other ways. Large crowds constantly made demands on Jesus and the disciples. At one point we read that "the crowd came together again, so that they could not even eat" (Mark 3:20). Limited private time for rest and sleep, for recreation and conversation, and for reflection and prayer would have taxed the body and spirit of these men. Furthermore, the insecurity of depending upon the hospitality of others for food and shelter, if not an actual lack of these basic necessities, surely added to the disciples' stress at times. Leaving family and home, to whatever degree each disciple did, would have taken an emotional toll. Also, the frequent and increasingly hostile challenges and criticisms from the religious leaders must have been difficult and exhausting for the disciples. On several occasions, at least some of the disciples witnessed events so profound that no doubt they were shaken to the very core of their being. While not questioning the rare and extraordinary privilege of following Jesus, we can see that the calling was costly in many ways.

On two occasions, physical and emotional exhaustion caused some disciples to be sleepy at inopportune times. In both cases, only Peter, James, and John had been invited to go with Jesus apart from the others.

The first time, they followed Jesus up the mountain where he was "transfigured," appearing in radiant glory alongside Moses and Elijah, with whom Jesus talked. As the event was described in Luke, "Peter and his companions were weighed down with sleep; but since they had stayed awake, they saw his glory..." (9:32). Imagine how tired these three men must have been, that under these circumstances they had to struggle to stay awake!

On the second occasion, Jesus asked these three to pray with him in the garden of Gethsemane. Surely the increasingly threatening environment in Jerusalem that week had been unusually stressful for them, and the just-completed Passover meal emotionally draining. The three disciples appeared, however, to ignore the effects of these circumstances and to overestimate their own strength and endurance. When Jesus returned after praying privately, he found the men asleep. Jesus obviously was distressed at his close friends' inability to pray with him. He addressed Peter sharply, "Simon, are you asleep? Could you not keep awake one hour? Keep awake and pray that you may not come into the time of trial; the spirit indeed is willing, but the flesh is weak" (Mark 14:37-38). Even this reprimand could not shake these disciples out of their sleepiness. Twice more on this occasion, Jesus found all three asleep. While sleeping instead of praying looks like a big mistake, soon the disciples made a bigger mistake when they failed accurately to count the cost and to evaluate honestly their ability to pay that price to follow Jesus.

Earlier that same evening, immediately following the last meal they shared, Jesus had predicted that the disciples would desert him. Peter, speaking with complete confidence, said, "Even though all become deserters, I will not" (Mark 14:29). Jesus told Peter that he would, in fact, deny him three times before the rooster crowed twice. Instead of trusting Jesus' wisdom and humbly asking for help, Peter was emboldened even further and reaffirmed his loyalty, saying, "Even though I must die with you, I will not deny you" (v. 31). Then the rest of the disciples claimed their allegiance to Jesus, affirming that Peter had spoken for them too.

Judas came later in the evening to identify Jesus to representatives from the chief priests who came to arrest him. Before Jesus was taken away, all of the disciples fled. They abandoned Jesus when following looked too dangerous, letting go of their confident commitment to follow him even to death. The cost of discipleship was suddenly very high indeed. We may wonder how much time passed before the disciples remembered what they had said earlier in the evening and what they had done as soon as they faced danger.

In the weeks ahead we will return to Peter, who denied Jesus, and to Judas, who betrayed him. For now, we see the disciples making a mistake in abandoning Jesus because they underestimated the cost of continuing to follow him and because they overestimated their ability to be steadfast in the face of whatever would come. No doubt their brave commitment never to desert Jesus reflected deep emotion, but perhaps little thought. Probably they had not considered the likely scenarios that could result from the hostile desires of the leaders gathered in Jerusalem, nor had they made an honest assessment of their willingness and ability to face death.

When Jesus called his disciples, he said, "Follow me." Those who accepted the call left all to follow. Their life with Jesus appeared to be a paradoxical combination of fulfillment and depletion. The costs—what they gave up and what they endured—were high.

Can we identify with these disciples who underestimated the cost? Do we need to? Are Jesus' requirements for his disciples *then* applicable to us *now*? Because we are not following Jesus literally down the road, we may think that we are not called to give up our house, our family, our career, or our possessions. More than likely we will not face crowds preventing our eating and sleeping, nor enemies threatening us because of our being disciples. Certainly we are not called to witness Jesus' arrest and at the same time risk our own. Can we accurately assume that discipleship is completely different now? Particularly during this season of Lent, we need to reflect on Jesus' statement about the job requirements: "If any want to become my followers, let them deny themselves and take up their cross daily and follow me" (Luke 9:23). This is a time for introspection into our lives as followers. If we are not incurring, or cannot even identify, any costs of following Jesus, then perhaps we need to examine the nature of our following rather than assume that the costs of discipleship are solely historical.

Some contemporary followers of Jesus do leave family and home to undertake missions that are physically and emotionally difficult. They sacrifice possessions beyond necessities and endure long, exhausting days in servant roles. A famous example is Mother Teresa, who spent much of her life responding to the overwhelming needs of sick and hurting people in India. Like Mother Teresa, there are people who may intentionally choose career paths that are more costly and less financially rewarding than other opportunities they might pursue. For example, a teacher may choose to take a job at a struggling inner-city school instead of accepting an offer from a suburban school in the upper-income neighborhood where he grew up. A woman finishing her post-doctoral work in epidemiology may decide to go to work in the mission fields of Africa rather than accepting an attractive offer to serve on the faculty of a prestigious medical school. A recent MBA graduate, instead of returning home to manage his family's huge farming enterprise, may choose to join the Peace Corps to teach farming practices and management in impoverished areas of Central America. Each person may be responding to God's call to minister to "the least of these." And like the Twelve, these contemporary disciples, while sacrificing so much, may yet find that they underestimated the costs of following.

What about the rest of us who may not think we are called to such obviously sacrificial service? Are we called to make any sacrifices regarding family, home, career, or possessions? Do we allow family members to control us or to put unreasonable limits on our time and opportunities for service to others? Perhaps we have so many places to lay our head—and within our own homes!—that we spend a considerable amount of our time and resources maintaining all of that well-appointed space. Our excessive hours at work may reflect a priority of achieving visible measures of "success." Dare we ask ourselves if we are "rich, young (or old) rulers" in our society? Certainly the answers to these personal questions are unique to each individual.

Surely the scene at Jesus' arrest is not at all applicable to us; or is it? Probably we will not be in a situation that closely, or even remotely, resembles the disciples' abandonment of Jesus. Perhaps, however, we may have an opportunity to take a stand with a person or on a principle in the face of criticism or even threats. What values does Jesus call us to uphold? Look around your community and consider what controversial issues could require your taking a costly stand as you try to be a follower of Jesus rather than a deserter.

Another helpful way to look at the cost of discipleship is to reflect on what denying self and taking up the cross might mean within our faith community. Perhaps we need to struggle together with the meaning of Jesus' words that his disciples must give up all their possessions, or the similar call to the rich ruler to sell all he had and to give the money to the poor. While I am not suggesting that the words be taken literally as applying to our faith communities in exactly the same way as they applied to the Twelve, some hard reflection does need to be done on what those words mean for us today. Also, our faith community may be an appropriate place within which to address where we think Jesus would have us stand on hard issues we face locally or nationally.

Before we can "underestimate the costs" of discipleship, we need to acknowledge that there *are* costs and be willing to undertake at least some of them. The disciples did underestimate the costs at times and fall short of being all that Jesus asked of them. Nevertheless, they recovered from their mistakes, and they kept facing the costs and trying to be faithful disciples. As you continue through this season of Lent, look and listen for the sacrifices God may be calling upon you to undertake—even if you, like the Twelve, previously tried and failed because you underestimated the cost.

Questions for Reflection and Discussion

1. Outline a job description for the twelve disciples called by Jesus, and outline also a job description for a disciple in the twenty-first century. Identify and compare the costs of discipleship then and now.
2. Cite an example of an individual or group in your faith community, or of someone you know elsewhere, who exemplifies the sort of bearing of the costs of discipleship that Jesus calls us to do. Have you done something that you or others thought was a sacrificial and costly act of discipleship?
3. Have you ever underestimated a financial cost—for example, of building a house, sending a child to college, or paying a remaining medical bill after insurance? Have you ever underestimated the cost of a commitment related to your discipleship? How did you resolve these problems? Compare your approaches to dealing with these different types of underestimating costs.
4. Reread Luke 9:23. Reflect on what the "cross" means in this context. What cross might you feel called to take up *voluntarily* on your path of following Jesus?
5. Think of persons in your lifetime who were arrested or faced persecution for taking stands that they understood as "standing with Jesus." What values were those persons trying to uphold? Do you feel called to an act of discipleship on a particular issue? What steps might you take? How might your actions be costly to you?

Prayer

We come before you, O God, claiming with confidence and pride that we are followers of Jesus.
He said, "Take up your cross and follow me."
Surely we did, O God, surely we did.

While on this Lenten path, we pause to wonder why we do not feel the weight of the cross.

Did we think Jesus said he would carry the load for us?

We pause again to ask ourselves if we are carrying a cross or believing in the cross or admiring the cross on the steeple.

We confess that we may have failed to pick up the cross Jesus showed us.

We are uncomfortable with this whole notion of carrying a cross.

Help us to wrestle with this call to voluntary sacrifice and meaningful discipleship.

Thank you, God, for your presence with us to strengthen, comfort, and guide us as we try to follow Jesus with our own cross.

Amen.

Focus for the Week

Reflect on what "one thing you lack" that Jesus might ask you to give up or to do before he says, "Then come, follow me."

Denial: I Do Not Know the Man

Scripture: Read Matthew 26:69-75.

The familiar story about Peter in the courtyard of the high priest following Jesus' arrest is found in all four Gospels. We know the basic facts: three times Peter denied knowing Jesus, and then the rooster crowed, just as Jesus had predicted. Peter made a big mistake, an infamous one. If we assume Peter's experience was unique to that time and circumstance, we may remain a detached observer of the events. Alternatively, putting ourselves into the story, we may be confident that if *we* were asked, "Do you know Jesus?" that *we* would respond emphatically, "Yes!" However, either of these reactions to the denial story may cause us too easily to shake our heads at Peter and his weakness. Before patting ourselves on the back, we need to pause on our Lenten journey to reflect more carefully on this mistake, lest we miss not only important details but also the relevance this significant story can have for our lives.

Understanding Peter in the courtyard requires first reviewing the hours earlier that evening. The disciples had gathered with Jesus for the Passover meal, sharing the bread and the cup before singing a hymn and going to the Mount of Olives. (See Matthew 26:17-30.) Jesus then informed the disciples that all of them would abandon him. Peter objected, claiming that he would never desert Jesus. After Jesus predicted even the timing of Peter's denial—before the rooster crowed—Peter boasted again, saying, "Even though I must die with you, I will not deny you" (Matthew 26:35). Although Peter was the most vocal in expressing his confidence in his own trustworthiness and courage, the other disciples joined in agreement with what we might imagine was a "one for all and all for one" spirit. So far as we know, none expressed reservations or reflected on how to prepare for possible danger.

Next, they went to Gethsemane, where Jesus asked Peter, James, and John to pray with him. As previously noted, all three men made a mistake in falling asleep instead of praying. When Jesus came to wake them a third time, Judas was arriving. He identified Jesus with a kiss before representatives from the chief priests arrested Jesus. The episode concluded with this significant report: "Then all the disciples deserted him and fled" (Matthew 26:56b).

Peter, however, turned back and went to the courtyard. Perhaps he volunteered, in yet another display of bravado, to return to learn what was happening and report back to the others. In fact, Matthew indicated that Peter "sat with the guards in order to see how this would end" (Matthew 26:58). While John's Gospel reports that an unidentified disciple accompanied Peter, the other Gospel accounts indicate that Peter was alone. When a servant girl accused Peter of being with Jesus, he responded, "I do not know what you are talking about" (Matthew 26:70). When another girl addressed her accusation—that Peter was with Jesus—to others in the courtyard, Peter gave a more forceful denial, saying with an oath, "I do not know the man" (26:72). When the bystanders accused him a third time of being "one of them," Peter both cursed and swore an oath, repeating, "I do not know the man!" (26:74). In the Gospel of John (18:15-18; 25-27), the phrasing of the questions almost begged Peter to deny the accusations. For example, a female guard asked, "You are not also one of this man's disciples, are you?" Peter agreed, "I am not" (v. 17). Although not all of his responses were blatant denials of Jesus, clearly Peter lied about his association with Jesus.

Possibly Peter's lies contained a measure of truth. As Peter watched Jesus' passive acquiescence in being arrested and his refusal to let his disciples resist, perhaps Peter wondered, *Why is he letting this happen?* Did he follow Jesus to the courtyard in hopes of witnessing some dramatic turn of events as Jesus used his wit and wisdom to win release? Peter may still have wanted Jesus to be someone other than who Jesus was called to be. Yet, when a disastrous end appeared increasingly likely, perhaps Peter thought, *I do not know this man*. Peter was right—he did not yet know Jesus. Probably no one really knew Jesus at that moment.

No doubt Peter hoped to be an anonymous eavesdropper and observer in the courtyard; but he got caught. Put on the spot and trapped in the courtyard, he panicked, lying out of expediency. Perhaps he thought that avoiding arrest—by whatever the means—was necessary to "help" Jesus. Because he did not listen to what he had been told by Jesus earlier in the evening or reflect on what he knew about the dangers in Jerusalem, Peter was unprepared. Given his physical and emotional fatigue, to hope to avoid his mistake, Peter would have needed a plan and probably the support of another disciple. He quickly got into a situation beyond his ability to cope. At the very first challenge—not by an armed guard, but by a servant girl—Peter reacted without thought, getting defensive almost immediately and making his biggest mistake.

We can almost hear the anger rising in Peter's voice as his first lie required another, and another. Why did he get so angry? One simple explanation is that the rising emotion within him in response to the threatening situation around him came out as anger. Anxious and defensive, Peter used oaths to add emphasis and weight to his lies, as if the sheer force of his words would convince those listening of his truthfulness. Perhaps instead, Peter was angry at himself for following Jesus to the courtyard. With little forethought as to what he was walking into, he was perhaps surprised by the unexpected challenges and quickly may have regretted being there. Alternatively, Peter may have been angry at Jesus. The disciples had attempted to protect Jesus from just this kind of danger. Repeatedly, he had rejected their concern. Peter may have resented Jesus' unwillingness to follow their advice. Thus Peter had plenty of anger to spill out when accused of being "one of them."

The other ten remaining disciples did not make Peter's mistake, because they were not there at all. Although Peter gets all the blame for what he did in the courtyard, he gets almost none of the respect due him relative to the others. Were Peter's verbal denials any more a rejection of Jesus than running and staying away as the others did? He deserves credit for having some combination of courage, curiosity, and concern that the others did not. At least Peter showed up.

What brought Peter back to being the disciple he had been called to be and wanted to be? The rooster crowed. (See Matthew 26:74-75.) Like a blaring wake-up alarm startling him into an awareness of what he had said, the crowing likely made Peter's stomach turn over and his heart break. Almost certainly the waves of guilt and regret crashing over him were emotionally devastating. When Peter remembered his response to Jesus' prediction, he surely felt disappointment, disgust, and even despair as he realized that he had failed Jesus and failed himself. He was not the courageous and faithful leader of the others or the follower of Jesus that he had proclaimed himself to be.

The account in Luke makes the scene even more poignant. We read that when the rooster crowed, "The Lord turned and looked at Peter" (Luke 22:61). What did Peter see? Perhaps Peter saw disappointment, yes, but also compassion in Jesus' face. If so, he may have felt a sharp sting in the depth of his heart and soul from being offered more than he deserved. Peter's painful regret is evident: "And he went out and wept bitterly" (22:62).

Only the writer of John told a story that provided insight into the process of recovering from this devastating mistake. (See John 21:15-19.) Three times, the post-Resurrection Jesus asked Peter if he loved him. Each time, Peter affirmed his love, and Jesus responded by calling Peter to take care of his sheep. Then Jesus repeated his very first call to Peter, saying, "Follow me" (John 21:19). To return to discipleship, Peter needed acknowledgement of his denial, forgiveness for what he had done, and restoration of relationship with Jesus. Being reassured that he was still the beloved Peter—called to follow Jesus and take care of Jesus' lambs—helped him move on to become a forceful leader in the early church. This story offered a valuable lesson in moving from denial to healing and wholeness.

We are invited to learn from all aspects of Peter's mistake—his overconfidence, his panic at being caught, his thoughtless and angry denial, his painful regret, and his restoration to discipleship. If we label Peter's mistake as lying when, having shown up exhausted and unprepared, he suddenly was questioned in a way that threatened him with imminent arrest, then perhaps we can identify more closely with him. Many of us have panicked when accused of some action we fear could get us into trouble. We do not want to face the consequences of telling the truth. Consider, for example, a teenager caught and questioned about coming in well after curfew or a college student asked about seeing a stolen copy of last semester's exam. Were you ever in a situation similar to one of these? Picture an office supervisor asking, "You're not the one who wrote those unflattering remarks about the company president on that blog, are you?" That question is in the form of those asked Peter, according to John's Gospel. How quickly and easily one says, "I am not," to avoid any trouble. Unlike these examples of risking punishment for inappropriate or forbidden behavior, Peter had not done anything wrong when he showed up in the courtyard. He took a risk in following Jesus, even at a distance.

We may identify with telling a lie—perhaps only a "little white lie"—when caught off guard. However, if pressed whether or not we might actually deny knowing Jesus, we still say, "I would never do that!" However, is denial always that obvious? Consider a possible scenario that at first may not appear to resemble Peter's experience. An office manager has befriended a recent legal immigrant who works on the maintenance staff in the office building. The manager offers to help the man's brother find employment without questioning the brother's documentation. However, at an office meeting the manager nods in agreement with a colleague whose solution to the problem of undocumented residents is to "round 'em up, lock 'em up, and send 'em back, no questions asked!" Is the office manager, in agreeing with his colleague, in effect saying about the maintenance worker, "I do not know the man"? Are we willing to stand up for someone if our colleagues, friends, or family put that person in a group whom they label as troublemakers? Do we deny Jesus if we turn our backs on our communities' "outcasts," folks similar to those with whom Jesus dined?

Was Peter's denial worse than our own? Perhaps we need to consider a prior question: Would anyone even have reason to say to us, "This man [or woman] is one of them"? (Mark 14:69). We will not be accused of denying Jesus if no one has any reason to think that we are his followers.

From Peter's mistake, we can learn how better to face risky situations we may encounter as we follow Jesus. Some may face considerable danger by, for example, working with a Christian relief agency in aiding refugees in a country hostile to ours. More of us may face risks in speaking up about potentially controversial church issues—whether to allow persons who are homeless to sleep on the downtown church property, or children of migrant families to use the church playgrounds and ball fields, or inviting Muslim and Jewish communities to partner in sponsoring a day of prayer. The risks in a hostile country are quite different from those in a disagreeable meeting within a church. Nevertheless, a wide variety of opportunities to act and speak in ways that affirm or deny our following Jesus come to us on an almost daily basis. We need to think about what we are facing, listen to good advice and clear warnings, and prepare ourselves for the difficult circumstances we anticipate. Remaining humble about our own ability to tell the truth and to affirm whom we follow when caught in a difficult situation may encourage us to be alert to risks and to be prepared.

If only Peter, instead of dismissing the possibility of making such a mistake, had been more attentive to Jesus' warning and had asked for help to avoid it. If he had kept Jesus' face in his mind's eye and Jesus' voice in his ears, perhaps Peter could have lived up to his pledge of never denying Jesus. If we can imagine Jesus turning and looking at us, as he looked at Peter, perhaps we can see our situations through his eyes and find the strength to say, "Yes, I know the man."

Questions for Reflection and Discussion

1. Read the full account of Peter's denial in each of the Gospels—Matthew 26:69-75; Mark 14:66-72; Luke 22:54-62; and John 18:15-18, 25-27. What new insights into this story have you gained from reading the Gospel accounts and from this week's discussion?

2. How might we exhibit denial of Jesus today? What are possible consequences of our denial? Have you been part of an experience where someone—perhaps you—in effect denied Jesus in words or actions? Explain your answer.

3. Jesus identified himself with the "least of these" and calls on us to stand with and for them too. Give specfic examples of groups of people in our society or around the world who have been denied recognition or rights or have been devalued in some way. How do we identify with and affirm the worth of all of God's children?

4. Peter is blamed for his mistake, unlike the other disciples, who did not show up at all following Jesus' arrest. Imagine the conversation when Peter was reunited with them. How do you

think the others might have felt? What might Peter have said to them, and how might they have replied to him? How do you think the disciples dealt with their guilt and despair?

5. Like Peter, to return to discipleship after a mistake, we need to acknowledge what we did, receive forgiveness, and be restored to wholeness in our relationship with others and with God. Consider beginning such a process this week with any untended mistake in your life. As you are comfortable doing so, share together within your group related issues or questions that weigh on your mind or heart, and talk about how you can support one another in addressing them.

Prayer

"Another servant-girl saw him, and she said to the bystanders, 'This man was with Jesus of Nazareth.' Again he denied it with an oath, 'I do not know the man.'"

—Matthew 26:71-72

We are confident, O God, that unlike Peter in the garden, we will remain faithful.
Our claims will always be:
We are with Jesus;
We know the man.
We are with Jesus in church on Sunday.
We read his words and sing his name.
Again we claim, we know the man.

God, are we missing anything?

Challenge us to listen carefully to Jesus' teaching and preaching and to look at his example.
Remind us that Jesus said to find him among the thirsty, the hungry, the strangers, the naked, the sick, and the imprisoned.
He called us to dine with sinners, to love our enemies, to be servants.

We pause to consider that maybe we have not been with Jesus.
We confess that we do not really know him.
Our grief at our denial, while not Peter's, is no less painful.

O God, let the rooster crow loudly and unmistakably in our ears. Startle us into honesty about our discipleship.

Forgive us, and help us find our own path of restoration to more meaningful relationship with Jesus.

Amen.

Focus for the Week

Look for ways to be a disciple so that you, like Peter, will be accused of being with Jesus, of being "one of them."

Betrayal: What Will You Give Me to Betray Him?

Scripture: Read Matthew 26:14-25, 47-56; 27:1-10.

Wthat is an act of betrayal? How is *denying* that we know
someone different from betraying that person? While
denial is often a defensive response to a challenge,
betrayal might be said to involve taking the initiative
to turn over someone or something to an "enemy." For example,
someone might betray a friend by revealing a confidence, a business
by selling company information to a competitor, or a country by giving classified documents to an enemy government. A betrayer's
motive may be to harm the one being betrayed, to aid the enemy, or
both. Alternatively, a betrayer may think he or she is acting in the
best interest of the betrayed.

In the Gospel stories, betrayal is readily identified with one person's act: Judas Iscariot's handing over Jesus to the religious author-
ities. Our operative word, *mistake*, may seem too gentle for what
Judas did. We prefer to put him into a special category of evildoers
and assume that we do not need to look for ourselves in *that* story.
However, if we look carefully at Judas and his mistake, we may identify a possibility for betrayal in our own discipleship.

From the first introduction to Judas in each Gospel, the reader is
alerted to his mistake. In Matthew (10:4), Mark (3:19), and Luke
(6:16), Judas is named last among the Twelve and labeled as the one

who betrayed Jesus. In John, the author informs the reader that Jesus was referring to Judas when, speaking to the Twelve, he said, "One of you is a devil" (John 6:70-71). The Gospel writers do not mention Judas Iscariot again until the week that ended with Jesus' death.

During that last week, according to John's Gospel, Jesus went to the home of Lazarus, Mary, and Martha for a dinner party. In this story, Mary anointed Jesus' feet with very expensive perfume. Judas, again identified as the future betrayer, criticized Mary's act by asking, "Why was this perfume not sold for three hundred denarii and the money given to the poor?" (John 12:4-5). Furthermore, the Gospel writer suggested Judas's motive, noting parenthetically, "He said this not because he cared about the poor, but because he was a thief; he kept the common purse and used to steal what was put into it" (12:6).

This account identified Judas as treasurer for Jesus and the disciples. Typically, that job would have gone to a trustworthy disciple. Yet, Judas was labeled a thief. The writer suggested that, instead of giving all the money to the poor, Judas would have kept at least part for himself. This event helped establish greed as Judas's motive in betraying Jesus. In a similar story in Matthew, however, *all* of the disciples were angry about the wasteful use of expensive ointment to anoint Jesus' head (Matthew 26:6-13). In this Gospel account, *all* thought that the ointment should have been sold and the money given to the poor.

Once in Jerusalem, Judas went to the chief priests and asked for money to betray Jesus to them (Matthew 26:14-16). The priests knew that Jesus was in Jerusalem. Why were they so pleased with Judas's offer? Timing was the key. They wanted to arrest Jesus when they could avoid stirring up the crowds, whom they feared (see Matthew 21:46). Judas received thirty silver coins—not a large sum. If greed was his sole motive, then surely he might have bargained for more. Nevertheless, he accepted the silver and immediately began to look for the right opportunity. (Unlike the Synoptic Gospel stories, the writer of John did not record any meeting between Judas and the high priests or any payment to Judas.)

Another possible motive for Judas's betrayal was that he hoped for, even expected, a kingdom ruled by Jesus in the more traditional sense of power and authority over others. Perhaps as they entered the threatening environment of Jerusalem, Judas felt pressured to take immediate action to force Jesus to declare his rule.

Ultimately, the Gospel writers turned to evil itself, personified in Satan, to explain the betrayal. For example, in John's Gospel, before the last meal that Jesus had with his disciples, we read, "The devil had already put it into the heart of Judas son of Simon Iscariot to betray him" (John 13:2). At the meal, after Judas received the bread from Jesus, "Satan entered into him" (13:27). Then Jesus said to Judas, "Do quickly what you are going to do" (13:27). None of the remaining disciples understood what this meant. They assumed Judas had been sent on some treasurer's duty of buying supplies or of giving money to the poor.

In Matthew's account of the Passover meal, Jesus said to the Twelve, "One of you will betray me" (Matthew 26:21). Immediately the disciples were "greatly distressed and began to say to him one after another, 'Surely not I, Lord?'" (26:22). Were they confidently affirming that they would never betray Jesus, or had Jesus' distressing statement raised questions in their hearts and minds? In either case, they did not express concern for Jesus, ask him what this meant and what might happen to him, or how they could be faithful to him. They did not challenge the group, asking the guilty one to confess so that they might work to restore honesty, trust, and unity. No, in their distress, each focused on himself. Out of insecurity, self-doubt, and worry, each wondered what he might do or whether Jesus suspected him. Although the other eleven disciples were not, so far as we know, contemplating any actions similar to Judas's plan, they may have been no less self-centered and self-absorbed.

According to the Synoptic Gospels, later that evening, Jesus was waking some of his disciples from sleep when Judas arrived at Gethsemane. Judas came with an armed crowd representing the chief priests and others. "At once [Judas] came up to Jesus and said, 'Greetings, Rabbi!' and kissed him" (Matthew 26:49). Then, the chief priests' delegates arrested Jesus. Judas was not mentioned again in the Gospels, except in Matthew.

A story of Judas's eventual fate (see Matthew 27:3-10) began with the reason for his change of heart: he "saw that Jesus was condemned" (v. 3). Judas returned to the chief priests to repent once he realized the outcome awaiting Jesus, whom Judas declared was an innocent man. The betrayer wanted to return the payment he had received and hoped, perhaps, to undo what he had done. His motivation for betrayal can be reevaluated in this light. According to this story, Judas did not want Jesus killed, nor was he so greedy as to want to keep the thirty pieces of silver.

In contrast, the priests, in responding to Judas's confession, said, "What is that to us? See to it yourself" (v. 4). Faced with his overwhelming guilt and grief, Judas threw down the silver in the Temple and "went and hanged himself" (v. 5). Perhaps Judas thought his death was the only way he could, or should, atone for his actions. Perhaps he needed so desperately to relieve his anguish from his guilt that he moved quickly to end his suffering. Although the inexplicable force of Satan working in Judas may be the best explanation for betrayal that we can identify, the story of Judas's immediate repentance does make us question evil intent.

In the minds of many Christians, Judas made the most tragic and despicable mistake in history. How might Judas have avoided the temptation to betray Jesus to achieve his own ends, whatever they may have been? Previously, we considered how Peter might have better prepared himself for the confrontation in the courtyard, so that he could have avoided doing what he so clearly did not want to do—deny Jesus. Like Peter, Judas had warning from Jesus about his impending mistake. While Peter forcefully rejected his personal warning, Judas seemed to ignore Jesus' predictions about his betrayal. If Judas had heeded the warnings and trusted Jesus enough to confide in him about his temptations, desires, and conflicts, perhaps Judas could have avoided his mistake. Alternatively, perhaps Judas thought he knew better than Jesus how to accomplish their ministry, as he understood it. If Judas had tested his agenda by conferring with the other disciples, then perhaps he would have realized that his plan was misguided. If he did talk with them and they dismissed his plan, Judas may have become more determined to prove them wrong. More likely, he isolated himself from Jesus and the other disciples and lost perspective about what might result from his actions.

Judas made another mistake after the betrayal, one that Peter did not make. After denying Jesus, Peter felt deep guilt and cried bitterly; but he turned around and walked back into relationship with Jesus. What Peter knew about Jesus allowed him to trust that grace and forgiveness were still available, even after denial. After betraying Jesus, Judas felt deep remorse, went to the priests, and offered restitution. Judas went to the wrong people to find what he needed. In his despair, he hanged himself. What Judas remembered about Jesus did not allow him to think that grace was still waiting for him, even after betrayal. We cannot understand fully why Peter returned to relationship and why Judas did not. Perhaps Peter knew Jesus in a way that Judas did not.

Are we likely to face circumstances in which we are tempted to betray someone close to us? Consider first those situations that present a conflict between our loyalty to a person and to higher values—values such as honesty, safety, or our love for that very person. For example, a young woman may feel betrayed by her parents who commit her to a drug treatment facility. An elderly man may think his children have betrayed him when they take his car keys away. Someone may betray a friend over gambling that has gotten out of hand, or a business partner for over-billing clients or padding expenses. These "victims" think that a family member, close friend, or associate has been disloyal in betraying the relationship, while the "betrayer" feels justified.

As we struggle to decide whether to act in such situations, to whom or what might we turn for guidance? If Judas somehow thought he was doing the right thing *for Jesus,* then certainly we recognize that discernment in these situations is difficult. If we think "betrayal" is justified, then before taking more forceful action, we should first confront the person, even if we have done so before. If we are met with denial or other resistance, a next step is to test our plan in an appropriate community or at least with a trusted advisor. Gather close family members to discuss a plan, or talk with a pastor, lawyer, doctor, or whatever person can best evaluate your situation. Try to separate self-interest from legitimate concern for the other person. Also, throughout the difficult time, talk with and listen to God, seeking wisdom, compassion, and strength.

Apart from these situations, where else might we experience or observe betrayal? Regrettably, acts of betrayal are so frequent in our society that often they are labeled with words less harsh and damning. For example, a man becomes romantically involved with an associate at work and thus betrays his wife. A member of the clergy betrays a community of faith by exploiting young people entrusted to his guidance. Politicians betray the voters who elected them when they take bribes or in other ways break the law. These and other acts of betrayal may reflect some of the same selfish motives we speculated Judas having, such as greed and the desire for power, or other motives including self-gratification. Given the long history and frequency of such betrayals, we must recognize that preventing them—perhaps even in our own behavior—is extraordinarily challenging. What, then, can we learn from Judas's mistake? Perhaps we can be warned to avoid the kind of isolation and secrecy that surely contributed to Judas's actions. Reflecting on our own values, being attentive to our emotions, communicating with our family and friends, connecting closely and honestly with our community of faith, and seeking help when troubled or tempted are all ways to help us avoid acts of betrayal. So far as we know, Judas did not do these things.

Finally, consider other ways that Christians may betray Jesus with actions contrary to his teaching and example. What acts might represent disloyalty or unfaithfulness to a commitment to follow Jesus that could, in effect, turn Jesus over to his enemies to be demeaned? If Christians publicly professing to be followers of Jesus accumulate material possessions and do not care for the poor; or demand cheap energy, food, and housing and do not protect God's creation; or vociferously pronounce judgment on and demand punishment for certain "sinners" while ignoring or excusing their own sins; or speak words of hate against people with whom they don't identify or with whom they disagree; are these Christians betraying Jesus? If we say that we stand for Jesus while doing these and similar things, are we turning Jesus over to his enemies who look at us, and then demean and dismiss him?

Betrayal is an ugly word for what is usually a harmful act. We do not want to see ourselves in Judas, not even a glimpse. If we are willing to look closely at Judas, we can understand better the mistake he made. Perhaps if we look more closely at ourselves, we can see our own inclinations toward betraying Jesus and can learn ways to avoid such potentially destructive actions. We may need to ask if our greetings to and affection toward Jesus are as hollow as those delivered by Judas when, "He came up to Jesus and said, 'Greetings, Rabbi!' and kissed him" (Matthew 26:49).

Questions for Reflection and Discussion

1. As we begin this Holy Week, read Mark 11, about Jesus' entry into Jerusalem and his experiences in the Temple. Sometime during this week, read Mark 14 and 15. What sorts of crucial mistakes did the disciples make during this final week? Also, look closely at Jesus as he moves from triumphant entry to suffering and death. Reflect on or discuss what sorts of feelings Jesus may have experienced during this time.

2. Has anyone ever accused you of betrayal? In what ways have you felt betrayed yourself? What emotions were present in these situations? What were the outcomes for each person and for the relationships involved? Were there moments, perhaps in the aftermath of the event, where God's redemptive and healing presence was felt?

3. How do you know when you are acting in the best interest of someone or when you are acting out of self-interest? List some guidelines that might be helpful in discerning the difference.

4. Betrayal is sometimes born out of isolation. How can we remain connected to our social or faith community when we disagree with what is being done or when we become isolated from it for other reasons? How can relationships be reestablished once trust has been violated?

5. Read again the last two paragraphs of this chapter. How do you react to this metaphorical description of betrayal of Jesus? Suggest other ways our thoughts or actions betray him. How might we discern which of our individual and corporate acts or omissions betray Jesus?

Prayer

We are eager, O God, to celebrate the triumphal entry into Jerusalem, to wave palm branches and shout "Hosanna!"

We wait impatiently to race to the tomb and shout, "He is risen!"

We confess that we are not so eager to face Monday through Saturday of this Holy Week.

We want no part of denial and betrayal, much less of suffering and death.

Help us to look at Jesus and to examine ourselves, as we continue our journey into the passion of this week.

As Judas betrays, the disciples flee, and Peter denies, trouble us to ask, "Lord, is it I?"

Forgive us for thinking that we can know Jesus and know your love, grace, and presence with us, O God, if we rush from shouts of praise to shouts of joy without experiencing the agony of these days.

Give us patience and courage to walk the final steps of this Lenten journey and to see the disciples' mistakes this week as our own.

Amen.

Focus for the Week

In humility, ask God to help you recognize your vulnerability to denying, or even betraying, Jesus by your words and actions. Pray daily for strength at this point of weakness.

Easter

Little Faith: Fear in a Storm and Doubt at a Tomb

Scripture: Read Matthew 8:23-27; Luke 24:1-53.

E aster Sunday is a day for celebration. Surely it is not a day to consider another mistake by the disciples, much less to reflect on "little faith." Yet, when we read the Gospel accounts about the last hours at Jesus' burial tomb and the first hours at the empty tomb, we see women followers of Jesus, not the eleven remaining disciples. When some disciples do show up, they doubt the women's reports or question what they see firsthand at the tomb. So, here at Easter, we consider the little faith of the disciples throughout the Gospel accounts. Our purpose is not to lessen our Easter celebration, but instead to deepen it.

In the Sermon on the Mount, Jesus addressed his listeners as "you of little faith" for worrying about food and clothing (Matthew 6:30). Noting God's provision of food for birds and "clothing" for flowers, Jesus said that worrying reflects "little faith" in God's care for us. Having "little faith" had nothing to do with any particular belief about Jesus. Instead, his message was about trusting—having faith in—God's love and providential care. Such care is not a guarantee that we will be protected from illness or pain or sorrow, any more than birds are protected from preying cats or flowers from late spring frost. It is a promise of God's presence with us throughout all our circumstances. On four occasions, according to Matthew's Gospel,

57

Jesus similarly accused the disciples of having little faith. We begin with these events before turning to the post-Resurrection stories.

On the first of two occasions involving a storm at sea, Jesus and his disciples left the crowd behind, boarded a boat, and sailed across the Sea of Galilee. Strong winds and high waves battered the boat, thus frightening the disciples. Jesus, however, was asleep. In their panic, the disciples rushed to wake Jesus, who asked them, "Why are you afraid, you of little faith?" (Matthew 8:26). Whatever the nature of the storm confronting the disciples and tossing them about, it had not affected the one to whom they turned for their rescue. Jesus quieted the storm. In the second storm, Jesus was not in the boat with the disciples. When he came to them, "walking on the sea" (Matthew 14:26), they thought they were seeing a ghost. Without mentioning their faith, Jesus comforted them, saying, "Take heart, it is I; do not be afraid" (Matthew 14:27). Soon, however, Peter jumped out of the boat to go to Jesus, began to sink, and cried, "Lord, save me!" (v. 30). As he reached out to Peter, Jesus said, "You of little faith, why did you doubt?" (v. 31). Focusing on whatever chaos swirled within and around him, Peter had little faith. He doubted God's presence with him to calm and support him. Once back in the boat with the rest of the disciples and with Jesus, calm returned and the storm subsided. Perhaps faith returned and doubt subsided.

By accusing the disciples of the mistake of "little faith," Jesus probably was not referring to their lack of certain beliefs about him or of an expectation of physical protection by him. Jesus never claimed any supernatural protection from danger and, in fact, intentionally avoided threatening situations on several occasions. Perhaps instead Jesus meant that they had little faith in God's desire to be present to calm and direct them in the middle of all of life's storms. Jesus may have been saying that faith in God's presence with them could have calmed their fear before the emotion took hold.

Our own fears amidst life's storms are not due to our failure, despite our best efforts, to believe rightly or "enough." Instead, our willingness to remember or to accept God's desire to be a calming and comforting presence with us amidst the threats may be closer to what "faith" means here. Faith may not require more effort on our part but may require less resistance to God's part. Again, this is not to suggest that faith provides protection from harm. Although Jesus referred to the "little faith" of those who are anxious about food and clothing, he did not say that having faith would prevent anyone from starving, including those in desperately poor, war-torn countries. He did not say that those with enough faith would not drown in a typhoon at sea. Faithful people do starve, drown, and die from injuries received in accidents or war. Faith in the face of fear is an inner reality for mind, heart, and soul, not a protective bubble for the body.

A third occasion of the disciples' little faith arose over their anxiety about what they would eat. After feeding over four thousand people and arguing with the Pharisees about signs, Jesus got into the boat with the Twelve and said to them, "Watch out, and beware of the yeast of the Pharisees and Sadducees" (Matthew 16:6). The disciples assumed Jesus was concerned because they had forgotten to bring more bread for the journey. Jesus responded to their worry, saying, "You of little faith, why are you talking about having no bread?" (16:8). He reprimanded them for their mistake and reminded them of his feeding thousands of people. How could they be anxious about what they would eat? Their little faith reflected a lack of trust in and dependence upon Jesus' provision.

In the fourth story, a father asked Jesus to heal his epileptic son, remarking, "I brought him to your disciples, but they could not cure him" (Matthew 17:16). As the Gospel writer tells us, Jesus healed the boy by casting out the demon that possessed him. Later, the disciples asked Jesus why they had been unable to heal the boy. He responded, "Because of your little faith" (Matthew 17:20). How can we understand the concept of "little faith" in the context of the disciples' inability to heal the boy? Certainly we would hesitate to assume that this story implies that contemporary "healers"—our doctors and other health care professions—who have enough faith, could cure any disease while those without faith could not. In considering the requirements for a "successful" healing, do we need also to consider the faith of the patient and of those who may be praying for the healing of the one who is sick? In fact, in Mark's account, the father of the boy acknowledged the problem of his own faith, crying out to Jesus, "I believe; help my unbelief!" (Mark 9:24). Obviously, understanding this story and finding meaning in the mistake the disciples made here is difficult.

In commissioning his disciples, Jesus gave them "authority over the unclean spirits" (Mark 6:7). One report indicates that the disciples had used this authority successfully: "They cast out many demons, and anointed with oil many who were sick and cured them" (Mark 6:13). We do not know what accounted for the disciples' "little faith" on this occasion that led to their failure to exorcise the demon from the boy. As they had been in the storm, and in worrying about their lack of bread, the disciples may once again have been anxious. Perhaps their desire to impress the crowd distracted them from compassion for the suffering boy and from being open to God. Such distraction might have limited their availability to be the means through which God's healing work could be done. This lack of trust in God's presence working in and through them was, perhaps, their "little faith."

Turn now to the four post-Resurrection stories, all of which point to the disciples' doubts. In Matthew, Mary Magdalene and another woman named Mary were the first to experience Jesus at the tomb. They were instructed to go and tell the disciples to gather in Galilee. (See Matthew 28:1-10.) The report of the experience of the eleven men who did gather there was contained in one verse: "When they saw him, they worshiped him; but some doubted" (Matthew 28:17).

In the longer ending to Mark, thought to have been added later to the original manuscript, Jesus appeared first to Mary Magdalene, who then told the disciples what she had seen. Later, Jesus appeared to two unnamed disciples, who also told the others. The other disciples did not believe these reports. Then we read, "Later [Jesus] appeared to the eleven themselves as they were sitting at the table; and he upbraided them for their lack of faith and stubbornness, because they had not believed those who saw him after he had risen" (Mark 16:14).

According to the story in Luke, the women at the tomb told the disciples what the angels had told them—"He is not here, but has risen" (Luke 24:5). However, the disciples did not believe the women. Peter did go to the tomb, and he left "amazed at what had happened" (v. 12), but exactly what he thought the empty tomb meant was not recorded. Next, following his appearance to two men on the road to Emmaus, "Jesus himself stood among [the disciples] and said to them, 'Peace be with you.' They were startled and terrified, and thought that they were seeing a ghost. He said to them, 'Why are you frightened, and why do doubts arise in your hearts?" (Luke 24:36-38).

Finally, among the several stories in the Gospel of John about

Jesus' post-Resurrection appearances is the two-part story about Thomas, who is known almost exclusively *because* of his doubts. Thomas was absent when Jesus appeared to the remaining disciples and "showed them his hands and his side" (John 20:20). Unconvinced when told of Jesus' appearance, Thomas said, "Unless I see the mark of the nails in his hands, and put my finger in the mark of the nails and my hand in his side, I will not believe" (John 20:25). He asked merely to see the same evidence that the other men had already witnessed. Thomas was with the others a week later when Jesus appeared again. Rather than reprimand Thomas, Jesus invited him to look and touch, getting whatever evidence he needed. Jesus told him, "Do not doubt but believe" (v. 27).

Each of these stories indicates that the disciples doubted, at least initially, that Jesus could still be known and experienced in life-changing ways. Our task is not to try to explain the inexplicable mystery and awe of these post-Resurrection experiences, but to see what we can learn from the disciples' mistakes. The disciples doubted not only the early reports from those who claimed to have seen Jesus, but also whether their own experiences were of the Jesus they had known. Were their doubts, and our own, *mistakes*? Is "doubt" synonymous with "little faith," the charge frequently leveled at the disciples by Jesus?

When the disciples doubted reports about the empty tomb, they were questioning the validity of the information. While readers of the Gospels may look at the disciples and think that they were doubting the most obvious and important of truths, we recognize that those men did not have the readers' perspective. While persistent doubt that rejects all insight into the truth may become a mistake, questioning facts or doubting what others tell us to believe is not a mistake and, in fact, keeps us in the tradition of the disciples.

Another aspect of their doubt coincides more closely with the notion of "little faith." Earlier we suggested that the little faith of the disciples usually referred to their lack of recognition of and trust in the presence of God with them to calm, comfort, strengthen, guide, and provide. In the Resurrection accounts, the disciples appear to doubt that the presence of God, which they had experienced working in and through Jesus, was still with them or available to them. Because of this doubt, the eleven disciples hid in fear and despaired over all they had lost, particularly Jesus, but also their vocation.

Perhaps they were full of regret, anger, or despair. This kind of doubt, had it continued, surely would have been destructive to the hearts and souls of these men. *This* is the doubt—their little faith in God's continued presence with them—that we label a mistake. The Gospel writers' stories of the post-Resurrection Jesus rebuking the disciples supports this label.

We have evidence that the doubts of some, if not all, of the eleven disciples were erased as each had his own experience of the resurrected Jesus. Again, we do not have to describe or understand the nature of their experiences to recognize that something caused a dramatic change in their lives. They were no longer disciples of little faith or doubt, but were men energized and filled with the spirit of God to continue the ministry that Jesus had begun with them. (See Acts, Chapters 1 and 2.)

The problem of little faith or doubt is not unique to the disciples, not even to Christians. It is a problem facing adherents of many beliefs. What can we learn from the disciples for our own struggle with doubt resembling the "little faith" of the disciples? Like them, we may be unable or unwilling to accept God's presence as calm in a storm. What if often we do not experience God as a real presence with us? What if we doubt that God *is*? The disciples were *with* Jesus and yet often revealed their little faith. They forgot or got distracted or lost their way and doubted over and over again the God being revealed to them. Throughout Jesus' ministry with them, and after his death and revealed presence with them again, still, they doubted.

If we follow in their tradition, we can expect at times to have "little faith," to doubt. As the disciples were proven wrong in their doubts and strengthened by their experiences, so too may we learn and grow from wrestling with our doubts. Perhaps the most important thing to learn from this mistake is that the disciples kept showing up to make the mistake again and again. Their doubts did not cause them to give up. They kept following Jesus and trying to be effective disciples even with their little faith. Consider also the journals and other writings of later Christians. Like the disciples, these men and women, through the times of darkest and deepest doubts, kept walking, kept writing, the next day and the day after that, and kept pouring out their little faith to the very One whom they doubted.

When the disciples lacked faith, Jesus acted to encourage and restore faith. Even though Jesus at times questioned and challenged them, he did not dismiss or condemn them. Most often he reached out to them, whether literally or figuratively, to reassure them and help them know that God was with them. On Easter, we celebrate the life of Jesus and our experience of him with us now. Even as we have walked through this Lenten season considering the cross and now arriving at the empty tomb, we may have been aware of our own "little faith." Picture again the story of Jesus reaching out his hands to rescue the sinking Peter, and of Jesus holding out his hands to reassure the doubting Thomas. Imagine Jesus reaching out his hands to you. He might say, "Do not be anxious, O you of little faith. God is with you, even when you doubt." Watch the disciples, learn from them, and keep showing up, constantly looking and listening for evidence of God's presence with you.

Questions for Reflection and Discussion

1. What situations cause you to become anxious and distracted from the awareness of God's presence? How does God reveal God's presence to you most clearly?

2. Describe a stormy time in your life when you experienced "little faith" or doubt. What were some of your thoughts or feelings? How was God's presence restored or reaffirmed?

3. Describe your reaction to the suggestion in this chapter that doubt is an inevitable and perhaps even necessary aspect of maturing in faith. How does this assertion fit in with what you have been taught about faith?

4. Mother Teresa's journals reveal persistent darkness and doubt even as she continued her work with the Sisters of Mercy among the poorest in India. How do you react to learning of such doubt in a contemporary saint?

5. Read Luke 17:5-6. Have you ever seen or heard of a mulberry tree moving in the manner described in these verses? If not, perhaps either no one has ever had such faith or Jesus was speaking metaphorically. How might you interpret what Jesus meant? Reflect on who we might be and what we might do if we had mustard seed-sized faith.

Prayer

O God, we have looked at the disciples and seen their mistakes, and our own.

We hear Jesus' reprimands and see his frustration and disappointment in them, and in us.

Help us to learn, not only from their mistakes but also from the most important thing that most of them did right—they kept showing up.

When insecure with what we have, distracted by success, overwhelmed by costly sacrifices, misguided in our plans, paralyzed by fear, defeated by our failures, and even lost in our doubts,

Remind us and strengthen us to keep showing up to accept your grace and to be guided as your beloved children.

Help us to show up this day, to be fully present with you, O God.

We pray for a moment when we can confess from the depth of our souls, "I have seen the Lord."

Amen.

Focus for the Week

Keep showing up as a faithful disciple with the assurance that, in spite of your mistakes and little faith, God is with you.